QUEENS OF THE ANIMAL UNIVERSE

BEE QUEENS

Rulers of the Hive

by Maivboon Sang

PEBBLE

a capstone imprint

Published by Pebble, an imprint of Capstone
1710 Roe Crest Drive,
North Mankato, Minnesota 56003
capstonepub.com

Library of Congress Cataloging-in-Publication Data is available on the Library of Congress website.
9781666343045 (hardcover)
9781666343106 (paperback)
9781666343168 (ebook PDF)

Summary: It's good to be a queen bee! The queen bee lets the other bees in the hive feed and care for her. What does she do? She lays eggs! A queen bee can lay more than 1,000 eggs a day! Take a look at the social structure inside a bee hive and the important role the queen and the female worker bees play.

Editorial Credits
Editor: Carrie Sheely; Designer: Bobbie Nuytten; Media Researcher: Morgan Walters; Production Specialist: Polly Fisher

Image Credits
Alamy: Chico Sanchez, 25; Getty Images: mady70, Cover, Paul Starosta, 27; Shutterstock: Ant Cooper, bottom 7, BrightRainbow, (dots background) design element, Daniel Prudek, top 7, Dave Massey, 19, Diyana Dimitrova, 10, DrSam, middle 7, Hand Robot, bottom 15, Imabulary, 28, Jay Ondreicka, 18, Kala Stuwe, 12, Kuttelvaserova Stuchelova, 8, 23, Lehrer, 5, Love Lego, 13, Michaelnero, 17, Mirko Graul, 20, Nadim Mahmud - Himu, top 15, Toms Auzins, 9, Volodymyr Burdiak, 21, WinWin artlab, (crowns) design element, Wirestock Creators, 11, Wulan Rohmawati, 29

Table of Contents

Words in **bold** are in the glossary.

Bees Rule!

Many animals live in groups. Often, males are the leaders. But this isn't always true! For social bees, females are in charge. While queens lay eggs, other females called workers run the bee group, or **colony**. Let's get the buzz on these busy female bees!

A queen honeybee (center) surrounded by worker bees

Meet the Social Bees

There are more than 20,000 types of bees in the world. Most kinds live alone.

Only a few types of bees live in colonies. These social bees include honeybees, stingless bees, and bumblebees.

Honeybees live around the world except Antarctica and the Arctic. Stingless bees live mainly in warm places. These places include South America, Africa, and Australia. Bumblebees live in North America, Central America, South America, Europe, and Asia.

Honeybee

Stingless bees

Bumblebee

Social bees live in nests. Nests above ground are sometimes called hives. Most bumblebees make their nests underground. Wild honeybees and stingless bees often make nests in rock crevices and holes in trees.

Honeybees gather outside their nest, which is inside a hole in a tree.

Most honeybees in the United States aren't wild. They are **domesticated**. People make places for the bees to build hives, such as boxes. People keep some of the honey the honeybees make.

Large earth bumblebees usually make their nests underground.

Bee Bodies

Bees are **insects**. They have three main body parts. These are the head, thorax, and abdomen. The wings are attached to the thorax. Bees have six legs.

A queen bee sits on a tree branch near smaller worker bees.

head

thorax

abdomen

Bumblebees and giant honeybees are the biggest social bees. They can grow to about 1 inch (2.5 centimeters) long.

Queens are the biggest bees in a colony. Their size helps them lay eggs.

The biggest type of bumblebee is the *Bombus dahlbomii*.

Bees eat **nectar** and **pollen** from flowers. A tube-shaped mouthpart called a **proboscis** suck ups nectar.

proboscis

Bees have five eyes. Two big eyes help them see bright colors. They use these eyes to find flowers. Three small eyes help them find their way around.

Bees have four wings. Their back wings are smaller than their front wings.

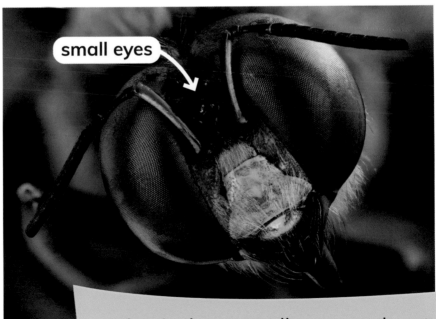

small eyes

A bee's three small eyes are located on the front of its head. The large eyes are on the sides of its head.

Home Sweet Home

Bee colonies are made up of a queen's sons and daughters. A bumblebee colony may have up to 400 bees. Honeybee colonies can have as many as 50,000 bees. Stingless bee colonies can have more than 100,000 bees!

Before a colony grows, bees need a safe place to build a nest. After one is found, the bees work together to build it.

Honeybee colony

Stingless bee colony

Honeybees build their hives from wax. The wax grows in their abdomen. They chew the wax. When it is soft enough, they can build with it. The bees make **cells** to hold eggs and food.

Bumblebees and stingless bees also make their nests with wax. Each type of bee makes a different type of nest. Some stingless bees build spiral hives.

Stingless bees on their hive

Every Bee Has a Job

How does a home with so many bees stay organized? Each bee has its own job.

The queen's job is to lay eggs. A queen honeybee can lay more than 1,000 eggs every day!

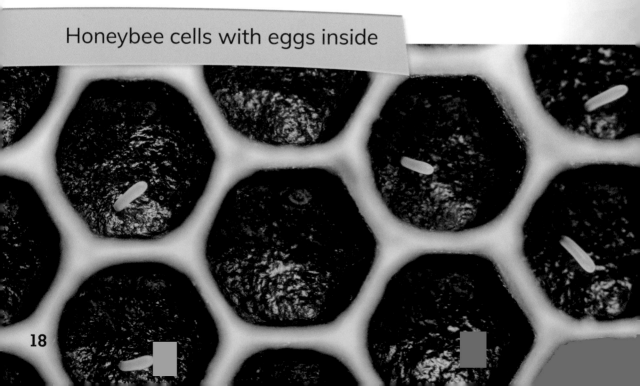

Honeybee cells with eggs inside

A worker bee collects food to bring back to the nest.

Worker bees have the most jobs. They build and repair the nest. They fly out of the nest to find and bring back food. They feed the young that hatch from the eggs. Workers defend their home too.

The job of drones is to mate. After mating, some drones die.

What kind of bee will come out of a cell? It depends on what it eats!

Workers feed young with royal jelly, honey, and pollen. Royal jelly looks like white snot. Only worker bees make it. A growing honeybee that is fed only royal jelly becomes a queen. Worker and drone young are fed royal jelly, honey, and pollen. Workers make honey from the nectar they collect.

royal jelly

Worker bees use wax to seal cells that are filled with honey.

There can be only one egg-laying queen at a time. When a honeybee queen dies, worker bees quickly start feeding some young only royal jelly. One of these bees then becomes the queen.

Stingless bees have unmated back-up queens in their nests. If the current queen dies, another queen mates and takes over.

New queens grow in bumblebee nests at the end of summer. The old queen dies, and the new ones live through the winter. In spring, they start their own colonies.

Workers surround and care for a honeybee queen throughout her lifetime.

Communication Counts

What's that smell? A queen bee communicates with other bees in a nest through chemicals. Other bees smell the chemicals and respond to them. For example, chemicals sent out by a queen honeybee can attract males.

Bees always know about their queen through smell. If a honeybee is removed and her scent disappears, every bee in the hive would know within 15 minutes.

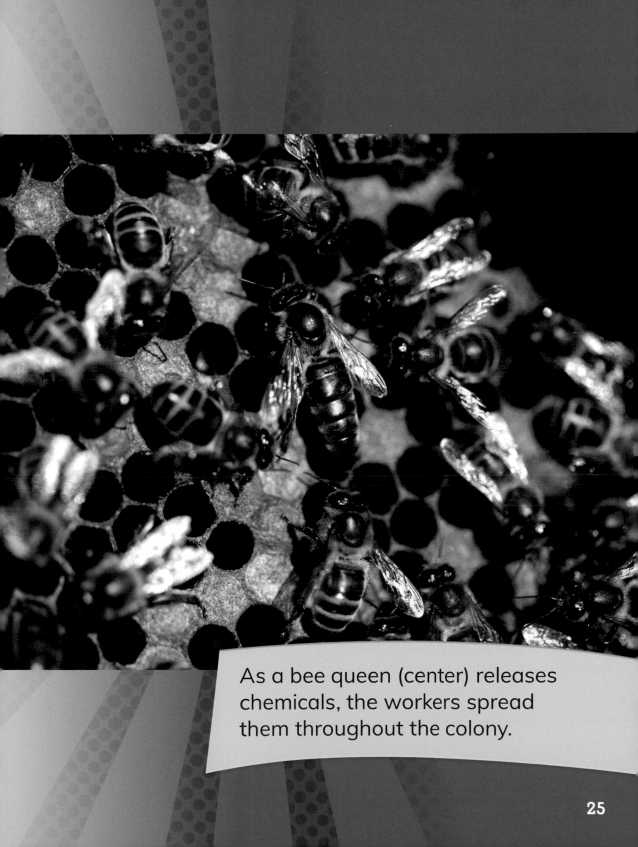

As a bee queen (center) releases chemicals, the workers spread them throughout the colony.

Twist and turn! Wiggle and waggle! A worker honeybee dances to tell other bees about the best places to find food. The dances tell the bees exactly where the food is.

Queens and the female workers are key to keeping a nest running. They help the colony survive. Female bees are amazing!

A worker honeybee with full sacs of pollen (center) does a dance to tell other bees where food is located.

Amazing Bee Facts

A honeybee doesn't taste with its mouth. It tastes with its **antennae**!

Bees have hair all over their bodies, even their eyes!

Honeybees are the most studied animals in the world, unless you count humans.

Honeybees vote on where to build their hives. When the majority of worker bees dance about the same place, they move.

Bumblebees don't die after using their stingers, unlike honeybees.

Unlike honeybees and bumblebees, stingless bees are active year-round.

Domesticated honeybees are moved all across the U.S. to **pollinate** crops. The bees carry pollen from flower to flower. This helps new plants grow.

Solitary bees are better pollinators than social bees. Pollen that collects on their bodies falls off their bodies better.

Honeybees can beat their wings up to 230 times per second!

Glossary

antenna (an-TE-nuh)—one of the feelers on an insect's head used to sense and touch smells; antennae is the word for more than one antenna

cell (SEL)—one of the compartments of a honeycomb; a honeycomb is a group of cells in a bee nest used to store food and eggs

colony (KAH-luh-nee)—a group of animals that live together

domesticated (duh-MES-tuh-kay-tuhd)—kept for use by humans

insect (IN-sekt)—a small animal with a hard outer shell, six legs, three body sections, and two antennae; most insects have wings

nectar (NEK-tur)—a sugary liquid created by flowers

pollen (POL-uhn)—a powder made by flowers to help them create new seeds

pollinate (POL-uh-nayt)—to transfer pollen from plant to plant; pollen makes new plants grow

proboscis (pru-BAH-skis)—a long, tube-shaped mouthpart; insects use this to drink plant juices

Read More

Fleming, Candace. *Honeybee: The Busy Life of Apis Mellifera*. New York: Holiday House, 2020.

Higgins, Melissa. *Buzzing Bees: A 4D Book*. North Mankato, MN: Capstone, 2019.

Johnston, Sharman, PhD. *Insects for Kids: A Junior Scientist's Guide to Bees, Butterflies, and Other Flying Insects*. Rockridge Press: Emeryville, California, 2020.

Internet Sites

Britannica Kids: Bee
kids.britannica.com/kids/article/bee/352839

National Geographic Kids: Honeybee
kids.nationalgeographic.com/animals/invertebrates/facts/honeybee

San Diego Zoo Wildlife Explorers: Bee
sdzwildlifeexplorers.org/animals/bee

Index

Author Biography

Maivboon Sang is a writer of short stories and nonfiction. When not writing, she enjoys working her way through pastry cookbooks. She lives in Minnesota with her husband who believes she makes too many desserts.